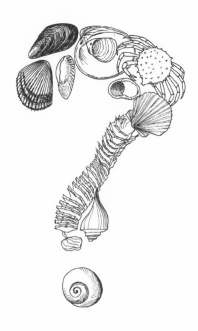

Paul Giambarba

What is it? at the Beach
on Cape Cod and the Islands

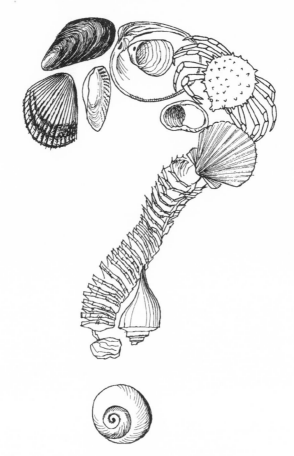

Written and Illustrated
by Paul Giambarba

The Scrimshaw Press

P.O. Box 1795, Mashpee MA 02649

Discover more about the subjects in this book at
www.scrimshawpress.com

Searching the Internet for more information

It's easy to find more visuals and details about each of the subjects in this book. There are any number of search engines you can use. If you are a beginner, connect with the Internet and keyboard in the name of a search engine. When its page comes up, type in the name of the subject you wish to search, such as any of those you might see on one of the following pages: mud snail, mud dog whelk, dog whelk, or the scientific names: *nassa, nassarius,* or *nassarius obsoletus,* depending upon how much you wish to narrow your search. When you are linked to a website you like , bookmark its URL so you can easily find it again.

Go to scrimshawpress.com for links and more information relating to the subject material in this book. Be sure to bookmark them, too.

For my granddaughter, Sofia

Printed and bound in the United States of America

Third, and revised edition, 2002

Contents

Introduction

The first edition of this book, *What is it? ... at the Beach,* was reviewed in *Scientific American* for February 1970. It came as quite a surprise to me. My book was described as "a rather personal guide to shore life [with] clear, outline drawings .... A single artist has done the job, working on paper with his pen, and photographic offset methods have brought us his work."

Thirty-two years later we can still say that a single artist has done the job, working now with a computer. The significant advancement is not so much being able to put all of the following illustrations and text camera-ready on a single CD and send it off in a number ten envelope to a printer, but in what the Internet has made possible, without charge, for so many of us.

Every common or scientific name mentioned herein has been, and can continue to be, searched on the Web and information updated. Instant results will often provide beautiful full-color photos of objects in their natural habitat, and – on occasion – even include streaming video of moving creatures.

My original intent in 1965 in publishing quality paperbacks at modest prices was also to provide stepping stones for readers who would wish to go on to the many excellent field guides that are available, such as that acknowledged below. I offer this book as a jump-start to that end.

Thanks to the marvels of technology, I have been able to update the original material from a wide array of sources. I am indebted to helpful Internet sources – and in particular – to the outstanding writing and illustrations of Kenneth L. Gosner in his *Atlantic Seashore, a Peterson Field Guide,* published by Houghton-Mifflin.

Life at the Beach

The beach varies from wet areas to quite dry. Plant and animal life change in these areas – each to its own adaptability.

The Sun

Energy from the sun causes vegetable organisms and tiny marine animals to grow.

The movement of the tides carries this rich food material throughout the sea where it nourishes other forms of life.

Dunes (dry)
Birds, barnacles, sand fleas

Upper Beach (Mostly dry)
Periwinkles
Limpets
Hermit crabs
Fiddler crabs
Whelks

Spring tides and storm tides occasionally reach this level

Normal high tide mark

Wet twice each day

Middle Beach (Mostly wet)
Starfishes, Worms, Mussels, Chitons, Anemones

Normal low tide mark

Lower Beach
Oysters, Crabs, Coral, Anemones

Unusually low tide mark

Offshore
Lobsters, Squid

This is the underwater world that is rarely exposed

Green Seaweeds

Beautiful Hair
Calothrix is a very common seaweed. Its color varies from yellowish to bright and dark green, and is very slippery when wet. Tiny threads, often transparent at ends, are found growing on other marine plants, rocks, and boat bottoms.

Mermaid's hair
Lyngbya is blackish-green, with long thread-like strands, matted together at its base. It is very common in summer on Cape Cod and southward along the Atlantic Coast.

Ocean Astroturf
Cladophora gracilis has bright, glossy and very fine yellow-green filaments, 4 to 8 inches, and loosely tufted short branches, common on wharves, pools, and eel grass.

Sea Lettuce

Ulva lactuca has an upper surface with folds, its underside is smooth. It has brilliant green leaves in various shapes from 4 to 24 inches. It is common just about everywhere.

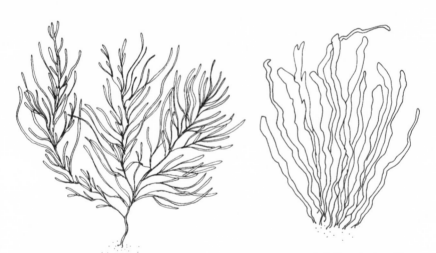

Enteromorpha compressa

is dark green, with long, slender branched and tufted fronds, 2 to 12 inches long, and sometimes as long as 24 inches. It is found everywhere.

Enteromorpha intestinalis

has yellowish-green, single, long, inflated fronds or tubes, often twisted and resembling intestines. It is found everywhere year-round.

Green Seaweeds

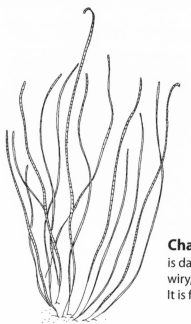

Chaetomorpha linum

is dark green, with five to twelve inch coarse, wiry, erect and tangled filaments. It is found in rocky pools.

Cladophora sericea

has dark green filaments, straight, tufted and stiff, five to ten inches long. It is common to the New England coast and found year-round.

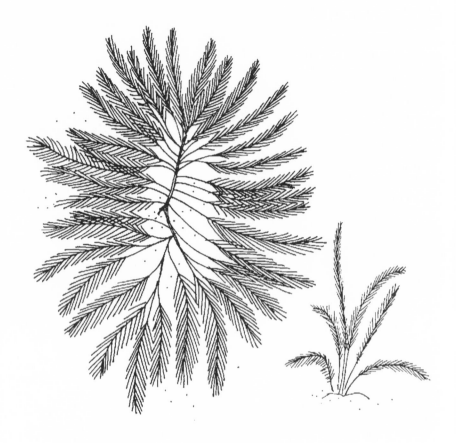

Sea Moss

Bryopsis plumosa is a dark green, bushy plant two to six inches long, with its fronds branched like feathers, tapering to the tip. It grows in tufts on rocks and piers at low water mark, and is common along the Atlantic shore.

Olive-Green and Brown Seaweeds

Desmarestia aculeata >

is spiny, with irregular branches, 12 to 72 inches long. It has bunches of yellowish hairs about one-half inch long when the plant is young. These fall off, leaving bare branches covered with spines. It is found just about everywhere.

< Chordaria flagelliformis

has slimy strings 6 to 24 inches long, blackish in color. Firm, elastic filaments branch out irregularly. It attaches itself by a disk to stones and shells, and is found along the Atlantic coast, common to New England.

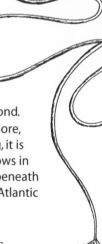

Mermaid's fishline >
or Smooth cord reed

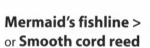

Chorda filum is a very smooth, hollow frond. It is brown, 12 inches to 12 feet long, or more, 1/4- to 1/2 inch in diameter. When young, it is covered with fine, transparent hairs. It grows in thick masses which can be seen waving beneath the water. It is common along the north Atlantic coast.

Brown Seaweeds

< Ectocarpus siliculosus
is brown in color, with dense and tangled tufts six to twelve inches in length. It has fine, interwoven filaments, and is found year-round.

Ectocarpus viridis >
has loose, very feathery brown tufts.

< Desmarestia viridis
has pale brown, feathery plumes up to 24 inches long, round filaments with many branches in pairs opposite to each other. It grows in clumps in tide pools and on rocks.

Bottlebrush >
Cladostephus verticillatus is brown, with bristly fronds covered with circlets of hairy branches. Looks spongy. Found on rocks along the Atlantic coast.

< Fingered kelp

Laminaria digitata has a stem one to five feet long, thick, round and leathery, with a hold-fast which resembles a claw. It gets its scientific name *digitata* from its finger-like form.

Broad Leaf kelp or Sugar kelp
Laminaria saccharina can grow many feet in length, with an undivided frond resembling a long tongue, and a wide, wavy margin. Its color is a semi-transparent olive-brown. it is found on the northern coast of the Atlantic.

Brown Seaweeds

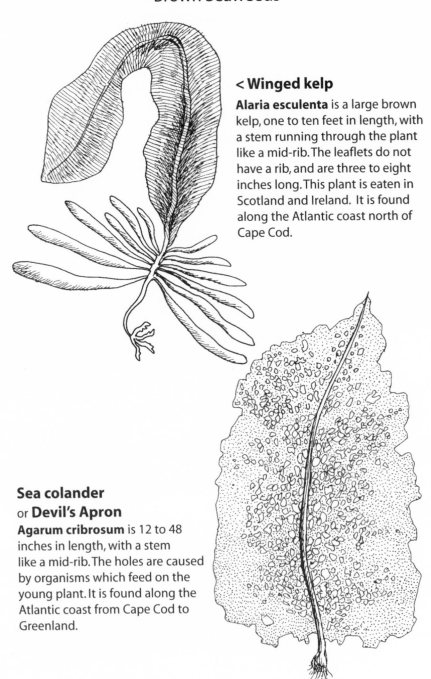

< Winged kelp

Alaria esculenta is a large brown kelp, one to ten feet in length, with a stem running through the plant like a mid-rib. The leaflets do not have a rib, and are three to eight inches long. This plant is eaten in Scotland and Ireland. It is found along the Atlantic coast north of Cape Cod.

Sea colander
or **Devil's Apron**

Agarum cribrosum is 12 to 48 inches in length, with a stem like a mid-rib. The holes are caused by organisms which feed on the young plant. It is found along the Atlantic coast from Cape Cod to Greenland.

Brown Seaweeds (Rockweed)

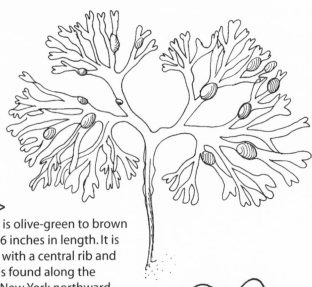

Bladder wrack >

Fucus vesiculosus is olive-green to brown in color and up to 36 inches in length. It is tough and leathery with a central rib and forked branches. It is found along the Atlantic coast from New York northward.

< Toothed wrack

Fucus serratus is used in Ireland and France for producing cosmetics. It has no air sacs. Its fronds have saw-toothed, or serrated, edges. It is found on the Atlantic coast, but it is not very common.

Horned wrack >

Fucus spiralis has a flat frond, and no air bladders. It is found from Long Island north to Newfoundland.

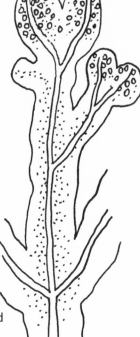

Gulfweed

Sargassum has about 150 species, most of which are found in warm seas. *Sargassum filipendula* has alternate branches, long narrow serrated leaves, and berry-like air vessels with long tips. The color is olive-brown, 12 to 36 inches long, or more. It is found along the Atlantic coast, from Cape Cod south.

< Knotted wrack
Ascophyllum nodosum
is the most common rockweed. except for Bladder wrack, or *Fucus vesiculosus* (see opposite page). It is long, dark brown and leathery, 12 to 60 inches long. Note its air sacs. It is found on the northern Atlantic coast from New Jersey northward.

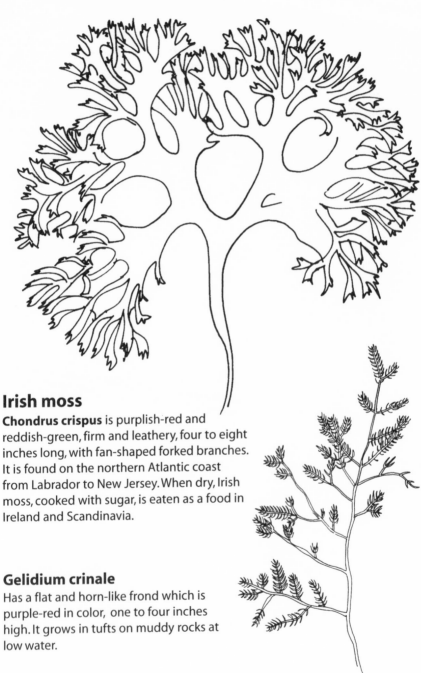

Irish moss

Chondrus crispus is purplish-red and
reddish-green, firm and leathery, four to eight
inches long, with fan-shaped forked branches.
It is found on the northern Atlantic coast
from Labrador to New Jersey. When dry, Irish
moss, cooked with sugar, is eaten as a food in
Ireland and Scandinavia.

Gelidium crinale

Has a flat and horn-like frond which is
purple-red in color, one to four inches
high. It grows in tufts on muddy rocks at
low water.

Red Seaweeds

Bushy red weed >

Cystoclonium purpureum is rose to dark purple in color, up to 24 inches long. It has a translucent main stem, irregular branches, with bladder-like swellings on some small branches. It is found along the Atlantic coast, from New York northward.

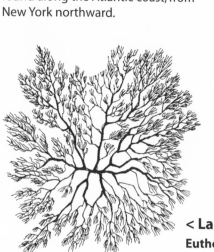

< Lacy red weed

Euthora cristata is bright red, two inches in size, with numerous spreading branches. It has no mid-rib or veins. It is found from the Arctic to Cape Cod.

Graceful red weed >

Gracilaria folifera is dull purple, four to twelve inches, with a short stem. The plants may vary, making identification difficult. It is common from Cape Cod south.

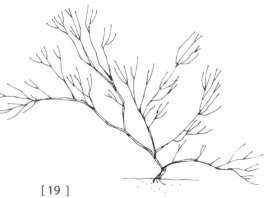

Red Seaweeds

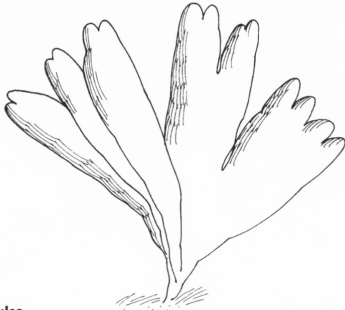

Dulse

Rhodymenia palmata is dark, purplish-red, six to twelve inches long, four to eight inches wide at the top. This fan-shaped plant grows on rocks below the low water mark. It is common to New England as well as the eastern Atlantic, and used as food in Iceland and cattle fodder in Scandinavia.

Polysiphonia

This species is tiny and pink, or reddish-brown. Over 200 types of polysiphonia flourish in warm, shallow water. It is bushy, with a thick, bristly stem and alternate branches dense at the ends. It is commonly found everywhere on stones at low tide.

Red Seaweeds

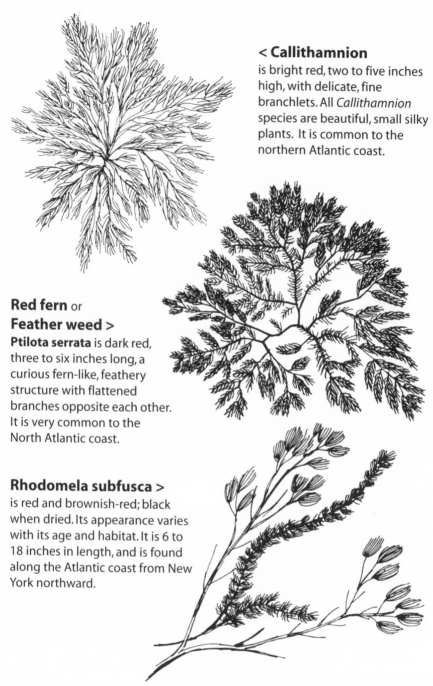

< Callithamnion
is bright red, two to five inches high, with delicate, fine branchlets. All *Callithamnion* species are beautiful, small silky plants. It is common to the northern Atlantic coast.

Red fern or
Feather weed >
Ptilota serrata is dark red, three to six inches long, a curious fern-like, feathery structure with flattened branches opposite each other. It is very common to the North Atlantic coast.

Rhodomela subfusca >
is red and brownish-red; black when dried. Its appearance varies with its age and habitat. It is 6 to 18 inches in length, and is found along the Atlantic coast from New York northward.

Red Seaweeds

< Red pitcher weed

Ceramium rubrum is three to eight inches long, variable in appearance with ring-like bands on its filaments. It is common everywhere and grows on everything.

Polyides rotundus

below, is dark red, three to six inches. Note repetition of forked branch pattern. It is cylindrical, and found in deep pools, along the Atlantic coast from New York northward.

< Common coraline

Corallina officinalis is about 1-1/2 inches long, variable in color from pale pink to deep purple, though the sun bleaches it white. It is rigid and feels like coral, and common to the Atlantic coast from New York northward.

Red Seaweeds

< Bangia atropurpurea
has dark purple filaments, one to six inches long, of fine hair-like texture. It grows on rocks and timbers, floats ashore in soft, silky masses. It is found on northern coasts of the Atlantic.

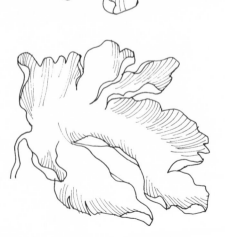

Porphyra vulgaris >
has variable shades of purple, and is three to twelve inches across the middle. It has a wavy margin, with many irregular folds. It is common everywhere. *Porphyra* is similar to green algae *Ulva*, except for its color. It is gathered and eaten in the south of Wales and the west of Ireland.

Porphyra umbilicalis is called Purple laver.

Porphyra laciniata
is different from *Porphyra vulgaris* in its margin, which is divided into narrow and ribbony segments.

Porphyra is edible. Chinese cooks make a soup of it.

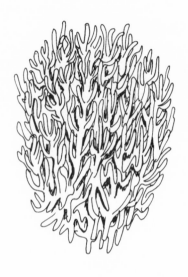

Finger sponge

Haliclona oculata is buff or gray in color when alive, yellowish-white when it is cleaned off and dried. It grows up to 18 inches tall, with clusters of slender branches varying in number. It is found along the Atlantic coast from Labrador to Long Island.

Red beard sponge

Microciona prolifera is orange-red when alive, grayish-brown and brittle when dry, with six to eight inch clusters of forked branches. It is found along the Atlantic coast from Cape Cod southward.

Crumb-of-bread sponge >

Halichondria panicea looks very much like its name, though colors vary from green to yellow and various shades of brown and orange. It is found washed ashore from Cape Cod to the Arctic.

Sponges

Sheep's wool sponge
Hippospongia canaliculata
or **H. lachne** is black in color when alive.
This is the best sponge found on the
American coasts. It is coarser than the
prized variety found in the
Mediterranean Sea. It's the old-
fashioned "bath sponge" used for years
before artificial sponges were made.
Sponge fisheries, located off the south
and west coasts of Florida, were once an
important American industry.

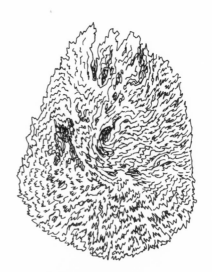

Yellow sponge >
**Hippospongia equina
elastica** is the second best
type of commercial sponge. It
grows with Sheep's wool
sponge, above, in two to
twenty feet of water. It is much
larger than the other varieties.

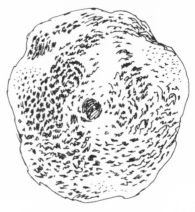

< Velvet sponge
Hippospongia equina resembles
brain coral in its texture. It has an
irregular shape, and is seven to eight
inches in diameter. It is also called
Honeycomb sponge for the way it
looks when cut in half.

Polyps and Small Jellyfish

< Club hydroid
Clava leptostyla grows on rockweed (*fucus*), the underside of stones at low water and in tide pools. It is red in color with tubes about 1/4 inch in height. It is common along the Atlantic coast from Long Island Sound southward.

Tubularia crocea >
has a red stem three to four inches in length. A cluster of reproductive buds hangs from inside its tentacles. It is found in bunches on piles and bridges in brackish water along the Atlantic from Cape Cod south.

< This is the stomach and mouth of the animal.

< Corymorpha pendula
looks as if it were a flower, though it is actually animal life. It grows up to four inches high, and is found from Cape Cod north.

Feather hydroid >
Pennaria tiarella has a black beaded stem, with red zooids found along the upper side of its branches. It is up to six inches high, and found among rocks and eel grass along the Atlantic from the coast of Maine southward.

Polyps and Small Jellyfish

< Sertularia pumila

is often mistaken for seaweed. It is the most abundant species along the Northeast Atlantic coast. *Sertularia* has a cup set against the stem instead of on stalks. The branches are 1 to 1-1/2 inches long. It is found on rocks and rockweed (*fucus*).

Nanomia cara >

is actually a free-swimming colony of animal life found along the New England coast. It has a hollow stem about three inches long, to which each individual animal is attached. At the top is the float, which propels the entire "jellyfish." Below its bells are three sets of zooids with tentacles.

< Bougainvillia superciliaris

is red, about two inches in height, with very slender stem and branches. It has eleven to fifteen tentacles per cluster, and is found attached to rocks and mussel shells in tide pools from Cape Cod north to the Arctic.

Jellyfish

These jellyfish are dangerous even when beached. Their dried stinger ends can be a problem if they become wet again.

< Portuguese Man-of-War

Physalia physalia has a float that varies in color from pink to bright blue. Along the top of the float is a sail, or crest. Long tentacles, up to 40 or 50 feet long, hang from the float. Some have stinging ends. Swimmers beware! Found along the Atlantic coast from Cape Cod southward.

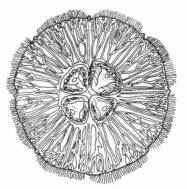

Moon jelly ∧

Aurelia aurita is bluish-white, transparent, and eight to ten inches across. Its short tentacles hang like fringe along its margin, which is notched in eight places. These are abundant on Cape Cod in spring, and disappear in July.

Jellyfish

< Red jelly or Lion's mane

Cyanea capillata is the largest jellyfish of all, growing from 1/2 inch to eight feet in diameter, with 100 foot tentacles in just six months! Most, however, are three to five feet across the top, with thirty to forty foot tentacles. It has a red disk with a white margin, and colored tentacles in eight bunches. It floats alone, and is common along the New England coast.

Swimmers beware!
Jellyfish can inflict severe pain with their stingers.

Purple jellyfish >
Pelagia noctiluca is a small jellyfish, only about two inches in diameter, pink in color with eight tentacles and four tails, about four inches in length.

Sea Anemones

Sea anemones resemble flowers and are many shapes and colors. They feed hungrily on small marine animals and shellfish. Their tentacles are used to sting their prey.

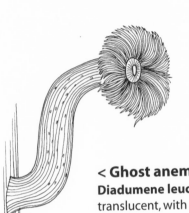

< Ghost anemone
Diadumene leucolena is pale and translucent, with a long, flesh-colored column-shaped body and white tentacles. It is found along the Atlantic coast mostly south of Cape Cod.

Burrowing anemone >
Haloclava producta is about six inches long, with twenty knobbed tentacles and twenty rows of warts. It is usually found buried in the sand from Cape Cod southward.

< Frilled anemone
Metridium senile is the largest and most common anemone, usually with a yellowish-brown or orange column. It grows up to four inches tall by three inches wide, and is found in tide pools at low water, from the Arctic south to Delaware.

Sea Corals

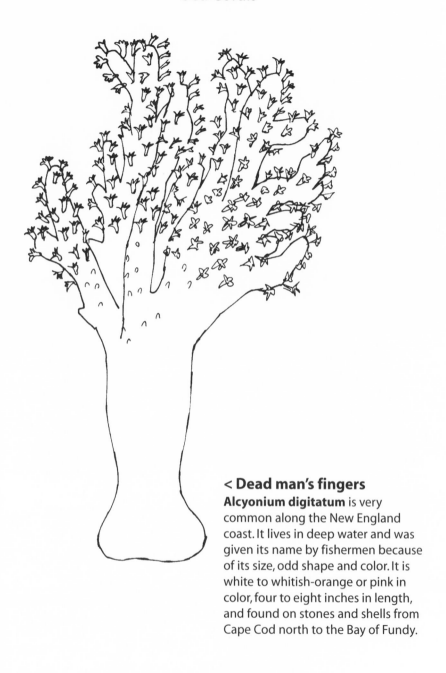

< Dead man's fingers
Alcyonium digitatum is very common along the New England coast. It lives in deep water and was given its name by fishermen because of its size, odd shape and color. It is white to whitish-orange or pink in color, four to eight inches in length, and found on stones and shells from Cape Cod north to the Bay of Fundy.

Worms

Lepidonotus squamatus >
rolls into a ball when disturbed. It is a
sandy-brown color, 1- to 1-1/2 inches
long, with broad, oval scales over its
body and head.

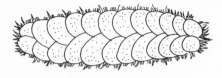

< Sea mouse
Aphrodita hastata is quite pretty,
iridescent in color, up to nine inches
in length. A furry coat covers its
scales. This worm lives in mud
below the limits of the tides.

Paddle worm >
Phyllodoce worms are about
three or more inches long,
about 1/8 inch wide, green
in color, with spots.

*Paddleworms are
found all along the
New England coast.*

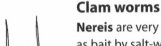

Clam worms

Nereis are very common, used
as bait by salt-water fishermen.
Nereis virens, left, is a dull blue-
green in color, sometimes over
18 inches in length. It leaves its
burrow to swim and feed at
night. It is found on the Atlantic
coast from New York northward.
Nereis pelagica, right, is colored
an iridescent reddish-brown. It is
common along the New
England coast. *Nereis* worms are
active and aggressive, with fierce
appetites. They are found
between tidemarks.

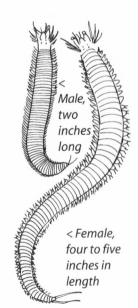

*< Male,
two
inches
long*

*< Female,
four to five
inches in
length*

< Plumed worm

Diopatra cuprea (head and part of body shown) is reddish-brown, speckled with gray, whitish opalescence and red gills. It is large, twelve or more inches long, with a flat body, very fast and hard to catch when pursued. It is found along the Atlantic coast from Cape Cod to South Carolina.

< Red-lined worm

Nephtys worms are whitish in color with a red blood vessel visible on their back sides. Eight to twelve inches long, with flat bodies, they are found along the New England coast.

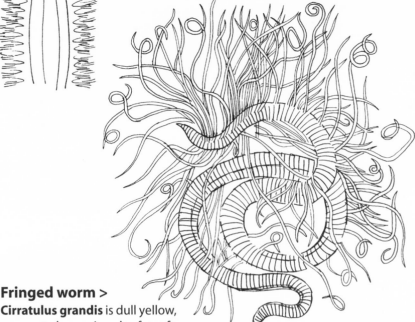

Fringed worm >

Cirratulus grandis is dull yellow, orange to brown in color, from four- to six inches in length. It has many long red or orange strings attached to its body which function as gills. It lies in mud or under rocks along the Atlantic coast from Cape Cod south to North Carolina. It has a round, cylindrical body.

Round Worms

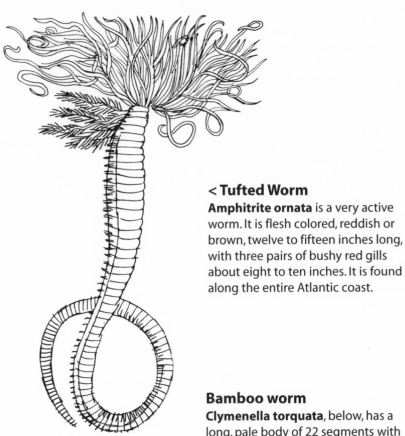

< Tufted Worm

Amphitrite ornata is a very active worm. It is flesh colored, reddish or brown, twelve to fifteen inches long, with three pairs of bushy red gills about eight to ten inches. It is found along the entire Atlantic coast.

Bamboo worm

Clymenella torquata, below, has a long, pale body of 22 segments with bright red bands. It is up to six inches and more in length. It builds straight tubes into sand, and is found on the Atlantic coast from Cape Cod to North Carolina.

Note collar on fourth segment
>

Moss Animals

Moss animals look like ferns, but are colonies made up of individual marine animals.

< Crisia eburnea

is a bushy tuft, ivory white, 1/2- to 3/4- inch high, that grows on algae such as red seaweeds. It is found in tide pools along the Atlantic coast from North Carolina to the Arctic.

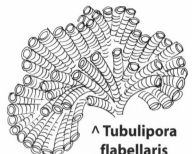

^ Tubulipora flabellaris

looks like coral, and attaches itself to algae in fan-shaped masses of long, crooked tubular cells, about one-inch wide.

Moss animal

Bugula turrita has yellow-orange to brownish branches, with dense tufts 3- to 12 inches long. It is common along the Atlantic coast. >

Eucratea chelata >

has a creeping stem, and branches of horn-shaped cells with holes on one side. It is found at low water on shells, stones, and rockweeds.

Lace coralline ^

Electra pilosa is a flat, whitish-gray colony up to eight inches wide with projecting hairs or bristles. It is found on stones, shells, and seaweed from Long Island to the Arctic.

Starfishes

Purple sun star
Solaster endeca is spotted red and purple on its upper side. It has a disk up to eight inches, with nine to ten arms. It is found from Cape Cod to the Arctic.

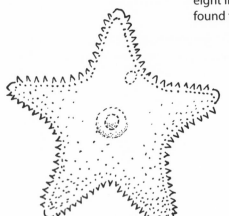

Mud sea star
Ctenodiscus crispatus is stiff, almost a pentagon in shape, and brownish yellow in color. It is about two inches in size, and found along the Atlantic coast from Cape Cod to the Arctic.

Starfishes and Brittle stars

Forbes asteria
Asteria forbesi can be bright orange with five tapered arms, about five inches in size. It is common from Cape Cod south.

Northern sea star
Asteria vulgaris is a similar species, common north of Cape Cod and pale yellow, though it may vary in color. This species is larger, up to eight inches in size.

Brittle Stars
will move around more than starfishes, and are harder to find. They will shed pieces of their arms when alarmed. They can lose their arms completely, but all will grow back.

Daisy brittle starfish
Ophiopholis aculeata (below) is spotted purple, with a spiny upper surface. The disk about 3/4 inch in size. It is found from Cape Cod north along the Atlantic coast.

Burrowing brittle starfish
Amphioplus abditus, above, is gray or brownish, with arms two inches long and a body about 1/2 inch in diameter. It is found burrowing into mud from Cape Cod south to Chesapeake Bay.

Sea Urchins

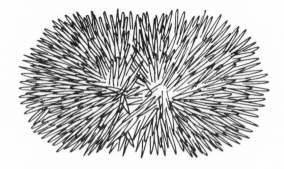

Green Sea Urchin

Strongylocentrotus droebachiensis is a very long
scientific name for the most common sea urchin of the
North Atlantic coast from Cape Cod north. Its color is
green, to greenish- purple, and its size is up to three inches
in diameter. The drawing below shows the shell of a dead
sea urchin with its spines removed.

Purple Sea Urchin

Arbacia punctulata is a small species, black, purple to
brown in color. Its body is up to two inches in diameter,
with spines, upon which it quickly walks along. It is
found from Cape Cod to Cape Hatteras.

Sand dollar >
Echinarachnius parma is purplish-brown when alive and covered with short, silky spines. It turns pale green when dead. It is about three inches in diameter, with a star on its upper surface. It is found along the Atlantic coast, from New Jersey northward to Labrador.

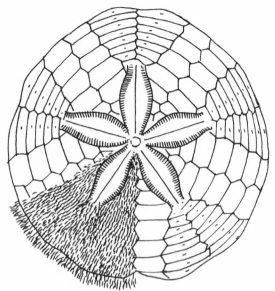

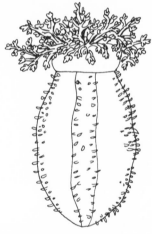

Sea cucumber
Cucumaria frondosa is dark purple or brownish-red on one side, a lighter shade on the other. It changes its shape readily, expanding from 15 to 18 inches in length. There are ten tentacles in its mouth. It is found from Cape Cod to the Arctic.

Red sea cucumber
Psolus fabricii is bright red, covered with overlapping scales and has a flat bottom. It is up to eight inches in size, and is found along the Atlantic coast from Cape Cod to the Arctic.

Crustaceans

Ship- or **Pelagic goose barnacle** >
Lepas anatifera has a bluish-white shell
about one inch long, and a grayish-brown
stalk from one to six inches in length. It
attaches itself to timbers and the bottoms of
vessels. It is commonly found everywhere.

Feather-footed shrimp
Mysis stenolepis is translucent,
about one inch long, with large
prominent eyes. It is found from
Cape Cod north.

*Common prawn, below,
is also called Common
shore shrimp*

Common prawn >
Palaemonetes vulgaris
has a translucent, spotted body,
1-1/2 to 2 inches long and is
found along the
northern Atlantic
shore.

Sand shrimp
Crangon vulgaris is 2 to 2-1/2
inches long. It is found all along
the Atlantic coast.

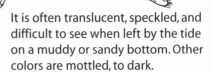

It is often translucent, speckled, and
difficult to see when left by the tide
on a muddy or sandy bottom. Other
colors are mottled, to dark.

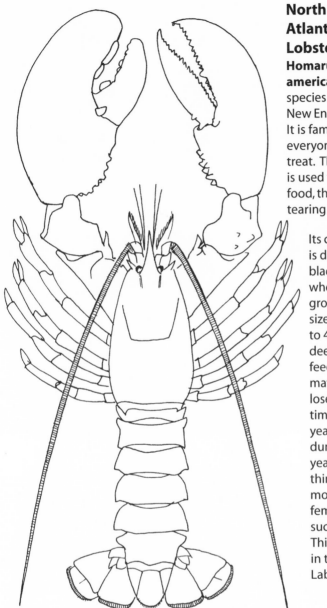

North Atlantic Lobster

Homarus americanus is the only species of lobster of the New England coast. It is familiar to almost everyone as a seafood treat. The large left claw is used for smashing its food, the right for tearing and cutting.

Its color, when alive, is dark greenish-black. It turns red when cooked. It can grow to a very large size and weigh up to 40 lbs. It lives in deep water and feeds on decaying matter. A lobster loses its shell eight times during its first year, five times during its second year, and three in its third year. Males moult twice, females once, each succeeding year. This species is found in the Atlantic from Labrador to Virginia.

Hermit crab

Pagurus arcuatus is the Hairy hermit crab of the Atlantic, dark-brown and hairy, with a carapace measuring about an inch or more. Larger, pink, and less hairy, is **Pagurus pollicaris**, Flat-clawed hermit crab. A tiny species is **Pagurus longicarpus**, or Long-clawed hermit crab, whose major claw is much narrower. A hermit crab backs into an empty shell in self-defense and adapts to wearing it if it should fit. It will look for another shell when it has outgrown its present home. It can change shells in a flash, and move rapidly even when carrying a shell on its back.

This is a hermit crab in a moon snail shell. The drawing, above, shows the hermit crab exposed without protection. Hermit crabs, described above, are all found on Cape Cod.

Crustaceans

< Mole crab

Emerita talpoida is not a true crab, and is often called a sand bug. It has a long, smooth, convex yellowish-white,1/2 to1 inch, body and tiny eyes on stalks, with a plume-like antennae. It is a fast digger, and is found from Cape Cod to Florida.

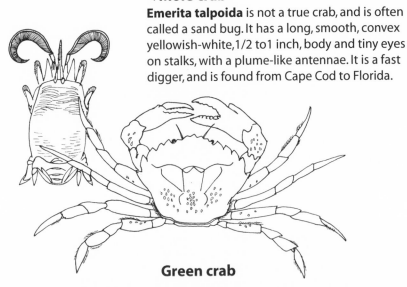

Green crab

Carcinus maenas is green, spotted with black, and yellow below. It is slightly over 3 inches wide by 2-1/2 inches long. Lively and aggressive, it is found along the Atlantic coast from Nova Scotia to New Jersey.

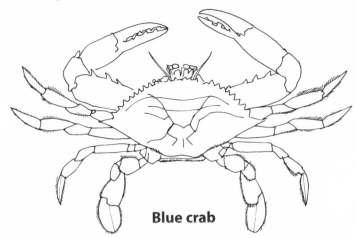

Blue crab

Callinectes sapidus has upper surfaces of gray or bluish-green, a lower body of dingy white and is up to nine inches wide and four inches long. Males have blue feet. It is found from Cape Cod to South America.
Be careful. It is very aggressive and it will bite!

Crustaceans

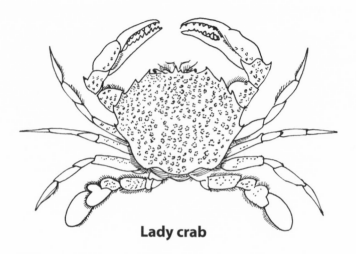

Lady crab

Ovalipes ocellatus is pale gray with small purple spots, up to three inches in size, and can be found along the Atlantic coast from Cape Cod to Florida. It is fast and nasty, so be very wary of its sharp pincers!

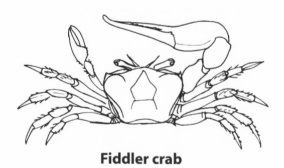

Fiddler crab

Uca pugnax is easily identified by the large claw of the male, which he waves about. It is a small brown crab, up to one inch wide, with long stalked eyes. Large colonies live in deep burrows in muddy banks and marshes along the Atlantic coast from Cape Cod to northern Florida.

Crustaceans

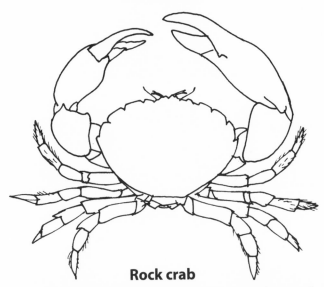

Rock crab

Cancer irroratus is yellowish-brown with red or purple freckles. This is slightly more than five inches in size. It steals bait and is a pest to lobstermen, but it, too, is now being sold as seafood. It is found from Labrador to South Carolina.

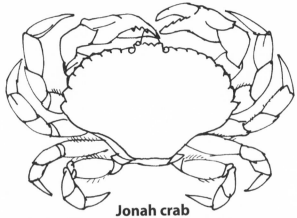

Jonah crab

Cancer borealis is similar to Rock crab, above, but larger; slightly more than six inches. It is harvested as seafood, and also found along the Atlantic coast from Nova Scotia to Florida.

Crustaceans

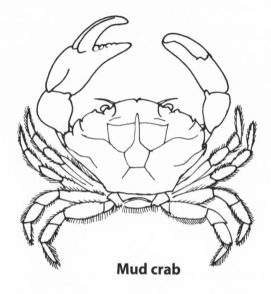

Mud crab

Eurypanopeus depressus is dark olive-brown with black claw tips, up to two inches wide and is found from Cape Cod to Florida.

Common spider crab
Libinia emarginata is small, dusky gray-brown, and is found in shallow water from Cape Cod southward.

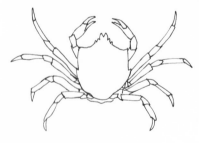

Spider crabs don't all look alike. They are slow and sluggish, and found in with seaweeds and marine organisms which they place on their backs as camouflage.

Crustaceans

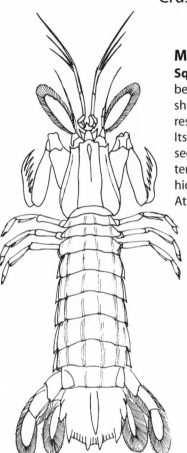

Mantis shrimp
Squilla empusa is a "thumb chopper" because of its dangerous claws. It is not a shrimp and gets its name from its resemblance to the praying mantis insect. Its color is pale yellowish-green with segments edged in dark green. It is eight to ten inches long and two inches wide, and hides in mud below low water along the Atlantic coast from Cape Cod to Florida.

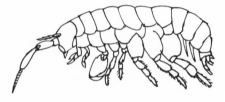

^ **Beach flea** or **Sand flea**
Orchestia agilis is brown, and about one-half inch in length. It jumps when disturbed. It is found from New Jersey north to Greenland.

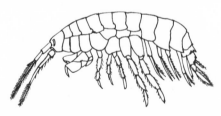

Scud >
Gammarus oceanicus is one of the largest amphipods, up to one inch long. It resembles a sand flea but does not jump. Reddish or olive-brown in color, it is found under stones and rockweeds near low water all along the Atlantic coast.

Crustaceans

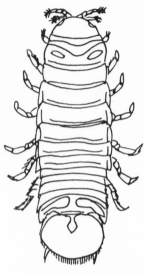

< Gribble

Limnoria lignorum is a tiny and ravenous destructive wood-borer, only about 3/16 inches in length. It can consume an enormous amount of material, and is often found on driftwood, between tidemarks along the Atlantic coast from Newfoundland to Rhode Island.

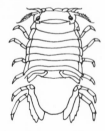

Lentil sea spider >

Anoplodactylus lentus is slim with long legs, about 1/4 inch long, found along the Atlantic coast from Cape Cod to the Caribbean.

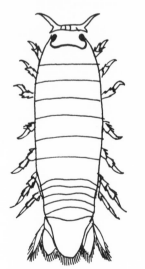

< Sea pill bug
Sphaeroma quadridentatum is gray, or variable, in color, and only up to 3/8 inch long. It rolls into a ball when disturbed. It is found from Cape Cod to Florida.

< Greedy isopod
Cirolana concharum is a yellowish bug-like creature about one inch in length. It is an isopod, or swimming marine animal that also attaches itself to objects. It is shy but it can bite, so handle with care. It is found from Cape Cod to South Carolina.

Crustaceans

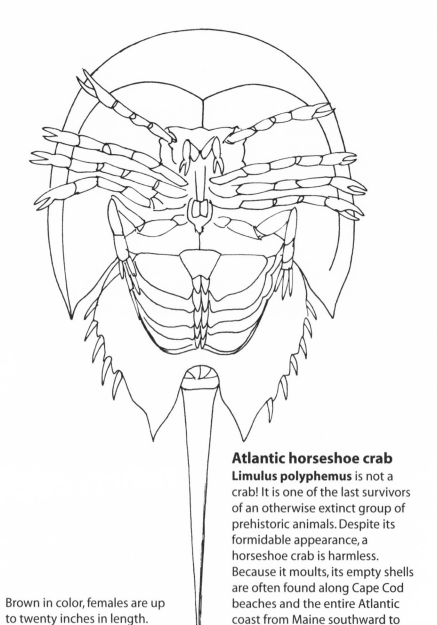

Atlantic horseshoe crab
Limulus polyphemus is not a
crab! It is one of the last survivors
of an otherwise extinct group of
prehistoric animals. Despite its
formidable appearance, a
horseshoe crab is harmless.
Because it moults, its empty shells
are often found along Cape Cod
beaches and the entire Atlantic
coast from Maine southward to
Mexico.

Brown in color, females are up
to twenty inches in length.

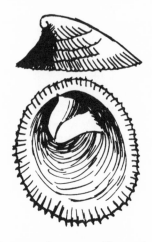

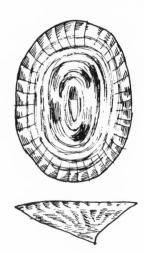

Cup-and-saucer limpet
Crucibulum striatum has a twisted tip in its bottom shell. It is about one inch in length, and is common along the New England coast as far south as Cape Cod.

Tortoise shell limpet
Acmaea testitudinalis has reddish-brown spots on a white surface. It is about one inch in length, and common along the Atlantic coast from the Arctic to Long Island Sound.

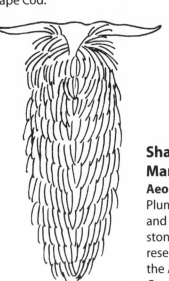

Shag-rug aeolis
Maned nudibranch
Aeolidia papillosa has also been called a Plumed sea slug. It is pink- or yellowish-gray and up to four inches in length. It is found on stones, piles, and algae, and when resting it resembles a sea anemone. It is found along the Atlantic coast from the Bay of Fundy to Cape Cod.

Mollusks

Pearly top shells

Margarites shells look a lot like periwinkles, and are up to one-half inch in size.

< Ridged top shell

Margarites cinereus is white, and in pale tints of pink and green.

< Greenland top shell

Margarites groenlandicus is reddish-brown.

Smooth top shell

Margarites helicinus has a smooth top shell, and is yellowish-brown in color.

Wentletraps

are found in mud or sand in shallow water, cast ashore after storms. The examples shown are sharply pointed, with rounded whorls and many ribs. Their length varies from less than one-half to one inch in size.

< Brown-banded wentletrap

Epitonium rupicola is yellowish-white with a touch of purplish-brown color and a dark brown band. It is found in sand along the Atlantic coast from Cape Cod to Florida and the Gulf of Mexico.

New England wentletrap >

Epitonium novangliae may have twelve ribs as well as spiral lines. Don't look for it on Cape Cod, however. Despite its name it is not found in these northern waters.

Mollusks

Northern moon shell

Lunatia heros has a heavy off-white, brownish shell, up to four inches in length. It is extremely greedy and feeds hungrily on live or dead fish. It is very common along the Atlantic coast from New Brunswick to North Carolina.

It lays its eggs inside a circular sand collar, often found on the beach

< Lobed moon shell

Polinices duplicatus has a flatter shell, smooth and polished. Its color is off-white below and light brown above, up to three inches in size. It is found along the entire Atlantic coast from Newfoundland to the Gulf of Mexico.

Easily identified by slipper or boat-like forms.

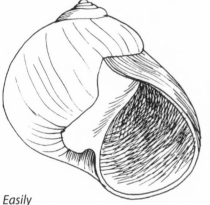

Eastern white slipper shell >

Crepidula plana has a white, flat, or concave shell and is more like a slipper than a boat. Both of these slipper shells are found all along the Atlantic shore.

< Common slipper shell

Crepidula fornicata has an oval dull white shell, faintly spotted with pale colors, and is less than an inch to two inches long.

Mollusks

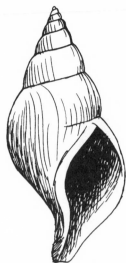

< Stimpson's colus
Colus stimpsoni is one of the most graceful of the larger shells of the Atlantic coast from Labrador south to the Carolinas. It is found in deep water and when washed up on the beach. It is three to five inches in size, and has a chalky-white shell.

Atlantic Oyster drill >
Ursoalpinx cinerea is dingy-gray in color and less than one inch long. It feeds on shellfish, particularly oysters, and is found along the Atlantic coast from Cape Cod to Florida.

Thick-lipped drill >
Eupleura caudata is similar in color and size to the oyster drill, but with a flatter shell. Also found along the Atlantic coast.

< Common Periwinkle
Littorina littorea has a thick shell with flat spiral ribs. Its color is dark, varying from black to reddish, with white inside the shell. It is up to just over one inch in length.

Rough periwinkle, Littorina saxatilis, right, is smaller, with white and yellow spots on an olive-green shell. It has a taller spire. Periwinkles are found along the Atlantic coast from Labrador to Maryland.

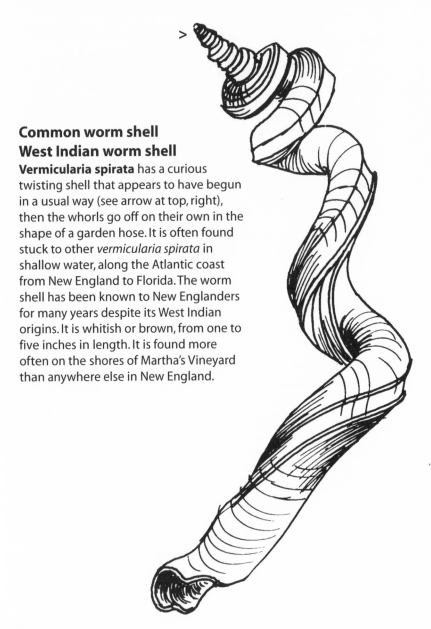

Common worm shell
West Indian worm shell

Vermicularia spirata has a curious twisting shell that appears to have begun in a usual way (see arrow at top, right), then the whorls go off on their own in the shape of a garden hose. It is often found stuck to other *vermicularia spirata* in shallow water, along the Atlantic coast from New England to Florida. The worm shell has been known to New Englanders for many years despite its West Indian origins. It is whitish or brown, from one to five inches in length. It is found more often on the shores of Martha's Vineyard than anywhere else in New England.

Mollusks

^ *This is the animal*

Mud snail
Mud dog whelk
Nassa

Mud snails are common all over the world.
They are found in large numbers on mud flats at low tide.

< Mud dog whelk

Nassarius obsoletus has a thick shell with
flat spiral ribs. Its color is dark, varying
from black to reddish, with white inside
the shell. It is up to one inch in length, and
found from Cape Cod to Florida.

New England dog whelk >

Nassarius trivittatus is smaller, up to
1/4 inch in size, with a thinner outer lip.
It is found all along the New England
coast to Florida. Dog whelks are
scavengers and feed on dead fish and
other sea creatures.

Red chiton

Ischnochiton ruber is our most
common chiton. It has reddish valves,
and an irregular pattern of white and
brown markings, and can be up to one
inch in size. This is a primitive mollusk,
found on the under side of rocks in cool
water, from New England to the Arctic.

Mollusks

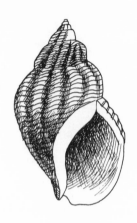

< Waved whelk
Buccinum undatum has a dull white shell up to three inches long, a yellow interior, and an outer coating, or epidermis, that is yellowish-brown in color. This is used as food throughout the world, and is readily found along the Atlantic coast from Cape Cod to the Gulf of Mexico.

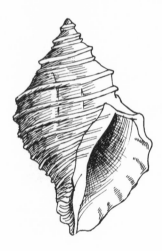

< Ten-ridged whelk
Neptunea decemcostata has an off-white shell up to four inches long, usually with ten reddish-brown spiral ribs. It is found along the Atlantic coast from Cape Cod north to Nova Scotia.

< Atlantic dogwinkle
Nucella or Thais lapillus is white, yellow, or brownish in color, up to two inches in length. The shell texture varies from smooth to rough. It is found along the Atlantic coast from New York northward to Newfoundland.

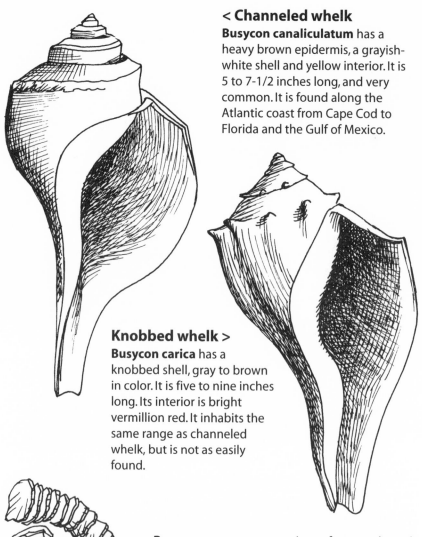

< Channeled whelk

Busycon canaliculatum has a heavy brown epidermis, a grayish-white shell and yellow interior. It is 5 to 7-1/2 inches long, and very common. It is found along the Atlantic coast from Cape Cod to Florida and the Gulf of Mexico.

Knobbed whelk >

Busycon carica has a knobbed shell, gray to brown in color. It is five to nine inches long. Its interior is bright vermillion red. It inhabits the same range as channeled whelk, but is not as easily found.

Busycon egg cases are strings of saucer-shaped disks, yellow in color. They are found along sandy beaches in summer and contain tiny whelk embryos. Knobbed whelk egg cases have square edges, as shown; channeled whelk egg cases have sharp edges.

Mollusks – Bivalves (2 shells)

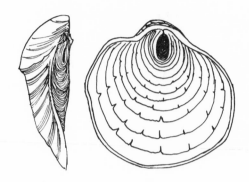

< Common jingle shell
Anomia simplex is shiny and scaly, in various shades of yellow, from one to three inches in diameter. It is very common, and found cast ashore on beaches along the Atlantic from Long Island north to Labrador.

Blood ark >
Andara ovalis is oval to round in shape, white, with a thick brown covering of its shell, up to two and sometimes three inches in length. Its blood is red and not colorless, like most bivalves, hence its popular name. It can be found from Cape Cod to the Gulf of Mexico.

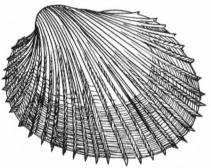

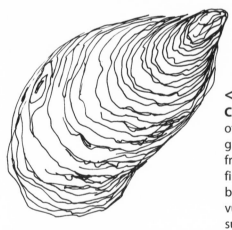

< Common eastern oyster
Crassostrea virginica has a rough, off-white shell with irregular shaggy growth lines. It is variable in size, from two to ten inches long. Oyster fishing and cultivation were once a big business, but oysters are vulnerable to disease and predators such as starfishes and drills. It is found from Maine and Cape Cod to the Gulf of Mexico.

Mollusks – Bivalves (2 shells)

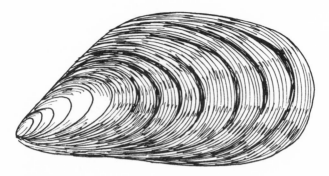

Blue Mussel

Mytilus edulis has a purple, sometimes brownish, shell with a dense, blue-black covering. It is two and one-half inches in length and very common along the New England coast. This is a seafood delicacy in France (*moules*) and Italy (*cozze*), which has found many admirers in the United States as well. Blue mussels are also cultivated in shellfish farms.

Horse Mussel

Modiolus modiolus is not shown. It is larger, up to nine inches long, with a deep brown covering and a red-orange animal found inside. It is also common to the northern Atlantic coast, but not found much south of Cape Cod.

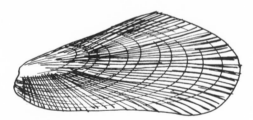

Ribbed mussel

Modiolus demissus has a dingy shell and pronounced ribs with a shiny greenish-brown covering. It is three to four inches in length, and silvery white inside its shell. It is found, usually in mud and muck, along the Atlantic coast from Cape Cod to Florida. *Don't harvest these mussels for food. They are not to be eaten!*

Mollusks – Bivalves (2 shells)

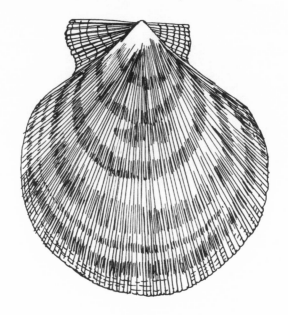

∧ Atlantic deep sea scallop

Placopecten magellanicus is light orange to reddish-brown in color, with bands of deeper color. It is from two to eight inches in size, with prominently raised ribs, taken by commercial scallopers along the northern Atlantic coast from Labrador to Cape Cod.

Bay Scallop ∧
Blue-eyed scallop

Aequipecten irradians is the shallow water species, the small succulent Cape scallop. Its color varies. It has about 20 ribs, and is up to three inches in size. It is found along the Atlantic from Cape Cod to New Jersey.

< Muscle

In America only the muscle of the scallop is eaten. Scallops jet-propel themselves along in the water by opening and closing their shells.

Mollusks – Bivalves (2 shells)

Giant sea clam or Atlantic surf clam

Spisula soldissima is a favorite food of gulls, who drop clams on rocks until they break. It is four to seven inches in size, with an off-white shell and a thin brown covering, and can be found all along the Atlantic coast to South Carolina.

< Hard-shell clam, Quahog, Cherrystone, Littleneck

Mercenaria mercenaria is up to four inches in size, has an off-white shell, and a pure white interior, sometimes tinged with purple. The shell was ground down and polished for wampum by Native Americans who called the clam a quahog, pronounced *ko-hog*. It is found along the Atlantic coast south from Cape Cod to the Gulf of Mexico.

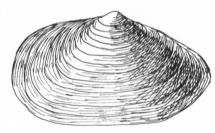

< Soft-shell clam

Mya arenaria is the steamer or fried clam of New England. It has a thin, off-white shell with a brownish covering, about three to five inches long, and is found in holes where it identifies itself by squirting water up through the sand or mud. It can be found along the Atlantic coast from Labrador to North Carolina.

Mollusks – Bivalves (2 shells)

< Common razor clam
Ensis directus is white in color, with a greenish or yellowish covering. It is up to eight or nine inches in length. It can move very fast and is able to dig into sand and be out of sight within seconds. It is common along the New England shore. Razor refers to an old-fashioned straight razor, which it resembles in shape and size.

Heart shell clam >
Northern cardita
Cyclocardia borealis has about twenty rounded ribs. It is about one inch by one inch in size and is found along the northern Atlantic coast from Labrador to Cape Cod.

Chestnut clam >
Astarte castanea is a small clam, only about one inch in size, with a thick, grooved shell and a brown covering. It is also found along the northern Atlantic coast from Nova Scotia to New Jersey. Look for it washed ashore on oceanside beaches.

Cross-hatched lucine >
Divaricella quadrisulcata is the small, thin *lucina* shell, about one inch in size with concentric growth rings. It is found along the Atlantic coast from Cape Cod to Brazil.

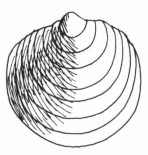

Mollusks – Bivalves (2 shells)

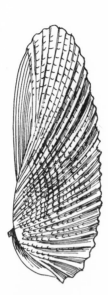

< Angel wing
Cyrtopleura costata is more wing-like and sculptured in texture than False angel's wing shell (right). It is white and four to eight inches long. It is found from Cape Cod to South America, but is not plentiful north of Cape Hatteras, NC.

False angel wing >
Petricola pholadiformis is dull white, only 1-1/4 to 2-1/2 inches long and marked in a ribbed manner. It is found along the Atlantic coast from Cape Cod southward.

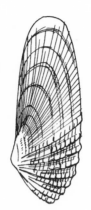

< Ship worm
Teredo navalis is extremely destructive. It burrows into submerged wood and destroys it. It doesn't eat the wood, but feeds on resident microscopic organisms. Worm-shaped but with a small bivalve shell at its large end, it is up to six inches long in northern waters, and 24 inches in warmer seas.

Atlantic long-finned squid >
Loligo pealei is from 12 to 24 inches long, white and speckled with color. It has large eyes and a triangular fin, and is the most common squid from Cape Cod to Cape Hatteras.

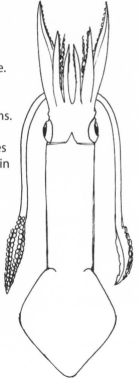

About the Author

Paul Giambarba began *The Scrimshaw Press* in 1965 to make available abundantly illustrated original material in quality paperbacks at modest prices. His mission: to write and illustrate books that would interest young readers in the world around them.

Giambarba received his training as an illustrator from Harold Irving Smith (1893-1967), a pupil of the great painter and teacher Robert Henri (1865-1929). As a designer for Polaroid Corporation, Tonka Toys, and others, he won many awards and international recognition for his work. He is also the author and illustrator of at least 18 titles published by *The Scrimshaw Press; Atlantic/Little, Brown; Houghton-Mifflin; Doubleday,* and others.

He has lived and worked on Cape Cod since 1960 and is presently an *RSVP* volunteer of the *Cape and Islands Senior Corps* sponsored by *Elder Services of Cape Cod.* For over 10 years he was a weekly contributor to Scholastic Magazines' classroom publications. Articles about him and his Scrimshaw Press have appeared in *American Artist* and *Horn Book* Magazine.